SECRET SOCIETIES

Mysteries and Conspiracies™

SECRET SOCIETIES

David Southwell and Sean Twist

ROSEN
PUBLISHING®
New York

North American edition first published in 2008 by:

The Rosen Publishing Group, Inc.
29 East 21st Street
New York, NY 10010

North American edition copyright © 2008 by The Rosen Publishing Group,
Inc. First published as *Conspiracy Theories* in Australia, copyright © 2004
by Carlton Books Limited. Text copyright © 2004 by David Southwell.
Additional end matter copyright © 2008 The Rosen Publishing Group, Inc.

North American edition book design: Tahara Anderson

Library of Congress Cataloging-in-Publication

Southwell, David.
Secret societies / David Southwell and Sean Twist.—North American ed.
 p.cm.—(Mysteries and conspiracies)
Includes index.
ISBN-13: 978-1-4042-1084-4
ISBN-10: 1-4042-1084-9
1. Secret societies. 2. Conspiracies.
I. Twist, Sean. II. Title.
HS125.S68 2008
366—dc22

2007010049

Manufactured in the United States of America

On the cover: *(Left)* Hooded members of the Ku Klux Klan meet around
a burning cross. *(Right)* Osama bin Laden founded the Islamic militant
organization al Qaeda in the late 1980s.

CONTENTS

1 AL QAEDA

It has become a sad fact of human history that major civilizations and powers seem to need to define themselves through conflict by those who oppose them. With the end of the Soviet Union it seemed as if Western democracies—especially the United States—lacked any opposition. Some academics even talked of an "end of history" and the era of unchallenged Western power. All of that changed on the morning of September 11, 2001. Within the hour between the first plane hitting the World Trade Center at 8:46 AM and the hijacked American Airlines Flight 77 crashing into the heart of American military power at the Pentagon, world history was forever changed and the USA had a new and deadly enemy to confront. Even before the twin towers of the World Trade Center had fallen to the ground, the terror network al Qaeda was already being mentioned by many informed commentators as the prime suspect behind the most devastating terrorist attack to have been launched in American history.

Osama bin Laden: mastermind or the mere pawn of secret masters?

Over the next few days, the public worldwide came to recognize and to dread the previously obscure al Qaeda and the face of its leader—Osama bin Laden. It soon became apparent that there was a vast terror network at large in the world with access to huge financial resources that was able to mount highly sophisticated terrorist strikes right in the heart of U.S. economic and military power. It was also apparent that al Qaeda and bin Laden had been known about by the U.S. intelligence agencies for several years. This was not least because they had played a role in funding al Qaeda and training them to fight since the early eighties when al Qaeda was at the forefront of frustrating the Soviet Union's occupation of Afghanistan.

The previous strong links between the CIA and the terrorists, especially the detailed knowledge held on members of its leadership, should have allowed the secret services an inside track on tackling al Qaeda. This campaign should have been in high gear after the United States blamed al Qaeda for turning on it with its bombing of the American embassies in Tanzania and Kenya and an attack on the USS *Cole* in Yemen. Many were surprised to find so little had been done to combat the growing menace of bin Laden and his gang between 1998 and 2001. Known supporters—including oil companies in which the Bush family had interests—were able to invest in U.S. companies, and al Qaeda members were even allowed to indulge in fund-raising activities while in America. It can certainly be argued that either al Qaeda was the cleverest terror outfit of all time or it was receiving support from forces with enough power to smooth its operations right under the noses of the U.S. authorities.

THE STRANGE PART

Italian newspaper journalists managed to discover that Osama bin Laden received treatment for a long-standing kidney condition at an American hospital in Dubai on July 1, 2001. They also obtained statements from witnesses who claimed that while in the hospital, bin Laden received several American visitors, including one known to have strong links with companies operating as CIA front-organizations in the strategic Gulf state. Given that he was already wanted by the U.S. security services for his role in terrorist activities against them in Yemen and the Gulf, why did they not use this opportunity to seize him?

THE USUAL SUSPECTS

The CIA

Having had a major hand in helping establish al Qaeda, it is not such a leap to believe that the CIA never completely severed its links with the terror outfit and that it continues to direct it from behind the scenes through its old best friend, Osama bin Laden. With a new enemy to fight and an open-ended war on terrorism to pursue, the power and the budget of the CIA seems set to last well into the future.

Major Oil Companies

Many of al Qaeda's original backers in the fight against Soviet forces in Afghanistan were from U.S. oil company backgrounds. Later, al Qaeda invested much of the money it made from the opium trade in Afghanistan back into U.S. oil companies. Given the impact that the war on terrorism has had on oil prices, possibly the real motive of al Qaeda and its corporate backers is something as simple as profit.

Saudi Arabia

Osama bin Laden comes from a dominant and well-connected Saudi family, and there is strong evidence to suggest that even post 9/11, powerful members of the Saudi royal family used their influence and wealth to protect al Qaeda members across the globe. Despite historically being a U.S. ally, al Qaeda may be a Saudi creation to extend their power under the guise of religious extremism.

THE UNUSUAL SUSPECTS

European Union

Whenever you start a close examination of al Qaeda, you begin to find a host of links between the terror network and individuals, companies, and security organizations based in the countries that make up the European Union—especially Germany. The possibility that al Qaeda is part of a shadowy EU agenda to destabilize its major Atlantic rival for global power should not be totally dismissed.

China

Worried about the problems created by growing Islamic nationalism in its outer provinces and wanting to take U.S. eyes off its growing military and economic power, the Chinese secret service could have infiltrated al Qaeda and turned it into an anti-American organization. While its two enemies fight a protracted and costly war, China can continue unmolested with its quest for global supremacy.

MOST CONVINCING EVIDENCE

There is little doubt that al Qaeda and those related to the family of bin Laden held a lot of sway in certain circles in the United States. On September 13, 2001—a day when all civilian air traffic in the United States was grounded—a charter flight left Florida, containing not only members of the Saudi royal family, but also members of bin Laden's family. The plane left an airport run by a defense contracting company with close links to the U.S. military, and bin Laden's family was accompanied by ex-security service agents. This suggests that far from being seen as enemies, bin Laden's people were treated as important and valued allies by someone with enough power in government to get them out of the United States before the authorities—especially the FBI—caught up with them.

MOST MYSTERIOUS FACT

Before September 11, former FBI deputy director and head of antiterrorism John O'Neill claimed that elements of the Bush administration were illegally negotiating with the al Qaeda–backed Taliban administration of Afghanistan. O'Neill resigned when nothing was done over his report that a giant American

oil company was trying to obtain permission to build a pipeline through Afghanistan to transport the large oil reserves of land-locked Kazakhstan. Sadly, he was killed in the September 11 attacks in New York City.

SKEPTICALLY SPEAKING

What is more unbelievable?—(1) The world is full of religious fanatics, some of whom have a hate for America in their hearts, or (2) there was plot to create an enemy for the only superpower left just so the marines had an excuse to go to foreign countries and kick butt? Hmm . . .

(Left) The Kaaba in Mecca, Saudi Arabia. Al Qaeda operatives have sworn to gain control of the most holy of Islamic sites.

2 FREEMASONS

Knock three times . . . The Masonic rites underpin one of the oldest, and certainly by far the most successful, of the secret societies.

Potential candidates—those who would like to be admitted—have to find a known Mason and ask, on three separate occasions, to be considered for membership. Only after the third request is the Mason allowed to acknowledge having heard the plea. Admission to the Masons is rigorously policed, and while any member is free to admit his own membership, he may not reveal any other member's name, or any ritual or decision internal to the craft. In this way, the Masonic rites have, for centuries, made sure that only the right people get in—but what sort of people are considered to be right?

Over the last couple of centuries, many groups and individuals have maintained that Freemasons are working to take over the world. There is no doubt that many important and influential people—politicians, policemen, judges, lawyers, cardinals and bishops, media tycoons, leading businessmen, celebrities, and so on—are Freemasons. Before his death, major conspiracy writer Bill Cooper claimed somewhat enthusiastically that, "The Masons are major players in the struggle for world domination." Many of his beliefs were based on fully provable links between the CIA, the Mafia, the Vatican, the British royal family, and Freemasonry. He also claimed it was possible to trace Masonic influence in the selection of political leaders of various ruling parties across the globe.

THE STRANGE PART

It may or may not be significant that the Masonic term for non-Masons is "Profanes," implying that the rest of us are less sanctified, or less holy, than they are. It seems a strangely intolerant term for what is a supposedly benevolent organization.

THE USUAL SUSPECTS

The Illuminati

The mysterious traditions in general, to which Masonry traces many rituals, frequently used the term "Illuminated" to refer to a person who was a member. This has been taken to signify a link to Adam Weishaupt's Illuminati, who were

officially announced to the world on May 1, 1776, in Bavaria, in present-day Germany. The Illuminati were supposedly controlling world events for hundreds of years before that date and are said to be still in power now. Could the Masons be under the control of the Illuminati?

The New World Order

Because their numbers include so many powerful people, the Masons are suspected by some theorists of being linchpins in the New World Order, the movement towards a unified, global population with no religion, a centralized government, and limited technology.

THE UNUSUAL SUSPECTS

Satan

The most popular accusation leveled at Masons is that they are in league with the devil. The hidden nature of their rituals, along with the occult imagery employed, has led many Christian groups to denounce Freemasonry as working for the forces of evil.

George Washington and the majority of the other Founding Fathers of America were high-ranking Masons.

MOST CONVINCING EVIDENCE

Former 33rd-degree Freemason Jim Shaw revealed in his book, *The Deadly Deception*, that even the supposed highest level of Freemasonry is just a lower rung for another Freemason-controlled pyramid-based power structure. Through his time as a high-ranking Mason, Shaw was able to gather convincing evidence that, at the levels kept secret from even Masons who think they are in control of the Brotherhood, there is a powerful group who have "gone higher" and really pull the strings of the secret society.

MOST MYSTERIOUS FACT

Despite the fact that some Masons claim the origins of the Brotherhood go back to ancient Egypt, there can be no doubt that the ceremonies of the Knights Templar had a huge impact on most of the rituals conducted within Freemasonry. However, the elements of Masonic ritual designed to allow a Freemason to control his emotions and energies to perform magical feats do seem to hark back to an even older period of history.

SKEPTICALLY SPEAKING

The great majority of Freemasons are respectable, upstanding professionals and business people with busy careers and family

It is easy to see why Freemasons are also known as the funny handshake brigade.

lives, and every year the Masonic lodges donate a fortune to charities and do charitable work. Many priests and vicars are Freemasons, and the order is open to all religions. It seems unlikely that so many decent people are in fact working for Satan, and it is certainly hard to imagine exactly how helping to organize a school rummage sale is playing straight into the hands of evil forces. Apart from anything else, Masons have no reason to support the dark side in the hope of gaining favor—most of them are already successful before they join.

Not only are the Masons probably one of the oldest and most successful secret societies, they are also the most-blamed by conspiracy theorists, which seems a little unfair given that they are ostensibly an organization devoted to charity, brotherhood, and the search for truth. But then, you don't know whether I'm a Mason or not . . . do you?

3 THE BAVARIAN ILLUMINATI

Adam Weishaupt was born in Ingolstadt, Germany, on February 6, 1748. Educated by the Jesuits, he became professor of natural and canon law at the University of Ingolstadt in 1775, at age twenty-seven, and was initiated into the Masonic Lodge "Theodore of Good Council" in Munich, in 1777. He was a cosmopolitan man who despised the bigoted superstition of the priests of his time. He decided to establish an enlightened—or Illuminated—society to oppose injustice, and this he did, forming the order that would become the Illuminati of Bavaria on May 1, 1776.

Originally called the Order of the Perfectibilists, its object was to allow its members to team up in order to "attain the highest possible degree of morality and virtue, and to lay the foundation for the reformation of the world by the association of good men to oppose the progress of moral evil."

ADAM WEISHAVPT.

In collaboration with a range of other influential figures, including Baron Von Knigge, Xavier Zwack, and Baron Bassus, Weishaupt developed an order that became extremely popular. Before long, some 2,000 people had enrolled as members. Lodges of the Illuminati were located in France, Italy, Poland, Hungary, Sweden, Denmark, Belgium, and Holland. The Bavarian authorities issued a suppressive edict concerning the order on June 22, 1784, which was repeated the following year in March and again in August. That same year, 1785, Weishaupt was stripped of his professorship and exiled from Bavaria.

Once it began to experience attempts at suppression, the order started to go into public decline, and by the end of the century, it had apparently vanished completely. The authorities illegally raided Xavier Zwack's home in 1786, and the documents that were seized were used to help suppress the order.

Most serious commentators take this decline at face value. The *Encyclopedia Britannica* barely mentions the Illuminati, and the vast majority of historical sources follow suit, judging the order to be insignificant. Others feel that the Illuminati disbanded into Masonry, a movement that was infiltrated in much the same way as cancer takes over a healthy body. Since that time, it is alleged, the Illuminati have stayed within the Masons, seizing power and manipulating the whole order.

Adam Weishaupt was alleged to have founded the Illuminati of Bavaria on May 1, 1776.

THE STRANGE PART

In 1906, the British Museum in London received a copy of a manuscript called "The Illuminati Protocols." These first appeared in Bavaria in the late eighteenth century, and Maurice Joly used parts in an 1864 play. The copy the British Museum received was written in Russian. It is also interesting that both Adam Smith's capitalist treatise *The Wealth of Nations* and that great democratic treatise the American Declaration of Independence were written in 1776. It has been suggested that Weishaupt may have been the mysterious Black-Cloaked Man who presented George Washington with the text of the declaration. It is also rumored that the raid on Zwack's house was spurred on by the chance interception in 1784 by the authorities of a document telling the head of the French Illuminati, Robespierre, how to orchestrate the French Revolution in 1789. Warnings were ignored, and the revolution happened on schedule.

THE USUAL SUSPECTS

Freemasons

To achieve their goal, the Masons knew their real target—overthrowing all world government and organized religion in order to allow peace and liberty to prevail—had to remain concealed. So, in order to avoid promoting hysteria against themselves, and as a way of dealing with criticism and exposé, the Masons created the Illuminati as a front organization to take the blame for any perceived misdeeds or shortcomings. It is a strategy that has worked brilliantly for two centuries.

THE UNUSUAL SUSPECTS

Robert Shea and Robert Anton Wilson

In the 1970s, Robert Shea and Robert Anton Wilson published a set of cult books called *The Illuminatus! Trilogy*. This was a story masquerading as the largest conspiracy theory ever seen, disguised as a grand exposé of the Illuminati. It is this book that has set the Illuminati back in the public mind. Of course, no one claims that the trilogy is anything other than a good work of fiction—or that Robert Anton Wilson is the current chief of the Illuminati . . . do they?

MOST CONVINCING EVIDENCE

In 1902 the Freemason William Westcott recorded receiving membership in the Order of the Perfectibilists from Theodor Reuss. Similarly, the occultist Eliphas Levi strongly connected the Bavarian Illuminati with Freemasonry in 1913.

MOST MYSTERIOUS FACT

Among the list of notable members of the Illuminati is the Marquis Saint Germain de Constanzo. This seems likely to be the Marquis de Saint Germain, the man most commonly suspected of being the only true immortal known in the world. He has cropped up as a sorcerer, an alchemist, and a wise man throughout medieval history. Who better to help found the world's most successful secret society?

SKEPTICALLY SPEAKING

There is, when you get down to it, no real evidence whatsoever to suggest that the Illuminati were anything other than a short-lived Bavarian secret society; it is just a lot of hearsay. If it hadn't been for *The Illuminatus! Trilogy,* the Bavarian Illuminati would still be an obscure sect lost in the footnotes of history.

4 THE KU KLUX KLAN

Nothing is more terrifying than organized hatred. The Ku Klux Klan has been among the most reviled of hate-fuelled organizations, spreading fear throughout the United States against minorities and those who disagree with the Klan's strict, racist views. Hiding behind anonymous white hoods, Klan members have become infamous for their burning of the Christian cross, their intolerance of racial integration, and their reputation for violence. In an age where so many inroads have been made to build bridges between races, the Klan still exists, proclaiming the power of white supremacy.

Rising in the ashes of the South, following the end of the American Civil War in 1865, the Klan came into being with a self-proclaimed mission to save the South from what it saw as the greatest threats of the time: blacks, Catholics, Jews, and the American federal government, among others. First led by Nathan Bedford Forrest, the Klan fought to preserve what it considered to be the purity of the white man. This was known as the Klan's first era, with Forrest acting as grand wizard.

By the 1920s, the Klan had grown in political power and entered its second era. Through the turbulent civil rights battles of the sixties, the Klan was implicated in murders and acts of violence against civil rights leaders and civil rights workers, especially in the South. Currently, the Klan considers itself in its fifth era, fighting not only for the white man, but to save all of Western civilization.

While the Klan is seen by many as nothing more than a hate organization run by ignorant men and women, it is possible that the KKK is far stronger, and has more influence, than is generally thought. Even today, when the civil rights battles of the sixties seem a lifetime away, when racism is fought and decried by so many, the power of hate continues to glow with all the intensity of the Klan's trademark burning cross.

THE STRANGE PART

Woodrow Wilson, twenty-eighth president of the United States from 1913–1921, once claimed that the Ku Klux Klan saved civilization on the North American continent. Why did he make this odd statement?

The burning crosses and hooded members of the KKK strike fear into minority groups across America.

THE USUAL SUSPECTS

The CIA and the FBI

The Klan has been implicated in the murders of popular black political leaders Martin Luther King Jr. and Malcolm X, apparently acting because both men posed a threat to the Klan's vision of America—a vision allegedly shared by many in the CIA and in the FBI. King's vision of peaceful racial integration was unpalatable, as was Malcolm X's more contentious view that blacks were superior to the white man in every respect. For refusing to conform to the Klan's ideal of a black man, both men were killed. In the case of King, Klan and FBI involvement seem particularly strong, since the FBI openly recruited Klan members before King's death.

Black Ops Race War

The KKK may be part of a race war directed against blacks and Jews, playing a role in the creation and distribution of the AIDS virus along with black ops government agencies. The Klan is also suspected of spreading false conspiracy rumors about ZOG (the Zionist Occupation Government), a purported Jewish plan to take over the United States. Such rumors help deflect attention from America's true enemy—the shadow government and its black ops agents.

THE UNUSUAL SUSPECTS

The New World Order

The Klan may be a front for the NWO, secretly furthering the aims of the New World Order while openly pretending to fight its influence on every level. This would include Klan involvement in the phenomenon of black helicopters, which, it is alleged, the Klan uses to incite panic in the populace and, the Klan hopes, will provide an environment in which it is easy to stir up racial tensions.

The U.S. Government

Despite recent liberalism in the U.S. government, many leaders in corporate, government, and military circles still favor a more conservative outlook, a viewpoint shared by the Klan. Funds could be diverted to the Klan, as well as weaponry and clandestine political support. This would explain David Duke's political career after he left the Klan.

Also suspected: the Bavarian Illuminati, the Order of the Green Dragon.

MOST CONVINCING EVIDENCE

The continued existence of the Klan in an age where hate groups are not tolerated suggests some high-level connection with the U.S. government. The American Constitution's guarantee of free speech as the right of every American is a guarantee that the U.S. government has shown in the past it will ignore as it sees fit (in the McCarthy era, for example). The Klan persists, and in the modern world, that poses the question of just who is looking out for its interests.

MOST MYSTERIOUS FACT

Former U.S. president Theodore Roosevelt once ploughed his own money into W. G. Griffith's film *Birth of a Nation*. Although now seen as a silent cinema classic, it is also clearly a pro-KKK piece of propaganda, which raises the question of why someone as powerful as Roosevelt felt it was right to fund the project.

SKEPTICALLY SPEAKING

You don't need a conspiracy to explain the ignorance that lies behind race hatred. Anthropology classes probably would not be a hit with the Klan, as the strong possibility that all humanity shares a common black ancestry might put a damper on cross-burning activities.

5 THE MAFIA

Since the start of the twentieth century, the Mafia has
constituted a significant part of the organized crime
underground in the United States. In addition to its
American operations, the Mafia is currently active in Italy,
southern France, Germany, and Russia. The facts of the
Mafia's presence and its wide range of criminal activities—
from prostitution and illegal gambling to drug distribution,
contract assassination, and slavery—are undisputed. What
is less well known is the extent to which the Mafia is one
unified organization.

The Mafia was first formed in the ninth century CE, in
Sicily. The original Mafia valued loyalty above all and
respected culture, family, and heritage. Membership was
only open to Sicilians, and the organization's aim was to
protect the interests of its members. As the centuries passed,
the Mafia evolved the belief that justice, vengeance, and

Knowledge of Mafia links to the Vatican are so well-known it even made it into the *Godfather* films.

honor were matters for the individual to look after and not responsibilities that should be delegated to the current government—which was often put in place by invaders anyway. Secrecy was maintained through the tradition of Omerta, which said that betrayal of the society's trust was repayable by death.

Early in the eighteenth century, the Mafia started to become openly criminal. Money was extorted from wealthy

Sicilians, who would receive a picture of a black hand. If cash were not forthcoming, arson, kidnappings, and murder would follow.

The Mafia has been active in the United States since the early nineteenth century, particularly in New Orleans. Word soon got back to Sicily that a lot of money could be made in the New World, and the organization grew swiftly. In 1924, prime minister and dictator Benito Mussolini cracked down on the Mafia in Italy, and many members fled to the United States. Ever since its super-profitable days of Prohibition, the Mafia has been spreading its influence throughout American political, legal, and financial institutions, skimming vast amounts of money in the process.

THE STRANGE PART

The Mafia in the United States is commonly thought to be a collection of rival gangs, clans that are organized on a family structure and have little but hatred for each other. However, this may be far from the truth. While the different gangs do certainly compete, the heads of the twenty-four families regularly meet in a cartel called the Commission. At these meetings, they settle territorial and business disputes, and decide policy for the coming months. It is possible that the Commission may also negotiate with government agencies, particularly the CIA, on areas of activity where mutual benefit can be derived.

THE USUAL SUSPECTS

The Network

Major world crime organizations are teaming up to maximize profits. Just like any legitimate big business, crime empires that merge activities can improve profitability. The Mafia has joined forces with the Triads, with the Yakuza, and with drugs cartels. This alliance, known as the Network, also accepts junior members such as Jamaican gangsters and Algerian slave traders. Because different groups control different resources, they have much to offer each other. The American Mafia, for example, can provide access to the U.S. banking industry, law enforcement, and justice systems as required.

Established Government

To what extent are government and organized crime actually different? Paying tax or protection money amounts to much the same thing, and few criminal organizations have caused as much public death as the United States did courtesy of Vietnam, or Russia did in Chechnya. Some conspiriologists believe that established governments actually control the Mafia as a way of having authority on the otherwise impossible-to-govern world of crime.

Heads of crime families, such as Sam Giancana, have even had presidents in their pay in the past.

THE UNUSUAL SUSPECTS

The Freemasons

The Mafia has long held strong ties to Masonry through the shadowy Vatican lodge P2, which is said to be the most powerful Masonic lodge in Europe. When Pope John Paul I determined to clear the Masons out of the Vatican—having discovered over 100 among the priesthood—he was killed, supposedly by the Mafia. Could the Masons be the power driving the Mafia's relentless advance over the years? Certainly both groups own a lot of judges and policemen.

MOST CONVINCING EVIDENCE

The spread of the Mafia is truly staggering. In the United States, the Mafia and officials from the government were maintaining an Illinois-based bank as a criminal enterprise, laundering money. The bank was run by an alleged Mafia associate, Catholic bishop of Cicero Paul Marcinkus. He was head of the Vatican Bank until 1991, working in association with a congressman who was a comptroller of the CIA's black ops budget.

A documentary detailing this was made, but before the program could be broadcast, state law enforcement officers threatened the filmmakers, their families were harassed, and one was falsely arrested.

MOST MYSTERIOUS FACT

The Mafia believes deeply in conspiracy theories. Some Mafia members even claim that the organization was originally formed to fight the mysterious "potere occulto," or hidden power they believe is rife in the world.

SKEPTICALLY SPEAKING

Organized crime is just that—organized crime. The last thing it wants to do, surely, is to take over the irritating trivia of everyday government, something that isn't necessary any-way, given the number of politicians already in the pay of Mafia dons.

6 MJ-12

In 1947, the now-famous crash of an alien spacecraft at Roswell, New Mexico, allegedly left the U.S. military in possession of a partly destroyed alien craft, along with several alien corpses.

The Roswell Air Force Base announced the discovery in the world's press. The story was retracted three days later, when the president, Harry Truman, suppressed the information in the national interest, remembering the panic caused by Orson Welles's famous radio broadcast *The War of the Worlds*. He assembled a group of twelve military, strategic, and scientific advisors to conduct a thorough investigation of the wreckage. This group was given security classifications above top secret and was named the Majestic Twelve, or MJ-12 for short. The craft was taken to the top-secret Nevada test area called Watertown, now known as Area 51.

From here, MJ-12 oversaw a number of different projects. In 1953 and 1954, President Dwight D. Eisenhower instituted

Evidence for UFOs keeps on cropping up. Is MJ-12 covering up the truth about alien activity on Earth?

Project Grudge under the auspices of Majority Agency for Joint Intelligence, or MAJI. Grudge was given a security clearance of MAJIC (MAJI Clearance), the highest security classification of all.

The work of MJ-12 is alleged to have led to the U.S. government signing a treaty with aliens to allow them to perform tests on animals and humans in return for technological information. MJ-12 also agreed to suppress all information regarding the alien presence and cover up the evidence of their tests, an operation known as Project Garnet. A further operation, Project Delta, was set up for this purpose and employs personnel to suppress, by any means necessary, evidence of alien presence. Project Delta provides the so-called Men in Black.

THE STRANGE PART

When an undeveloped roll of film containing images of files purporting to be a presidential briefing concerning MJ-12 turned up out of the blue in the mailbox of a prominent UFO researcher, many people were quick to dismiss the documents as fakes. However, as more investigation was made into the claims of the so-called MJ-12 documents, it became harder to dismiss them, as they identified the only days possible when all the twelve original members could have met for meetings—a level of detail unlikely in a hoax.

THE USUAL SUSPECTS

The U.S. Military

Always known for being pragmatic, the military supports MJ-12 recognizing that although the aliens may not be a good thing, there is little that can be done to change matters. While research into weapons with which to fight the aliens continues, MJ-12 can only stick to its end of the bargain in order to prevent the invaders taking matters into their own hands. Better a few missing abductees and a few murdered UFO investigators than the human race enslaved.

Majesty

MJ-12 is not in control at all. That dubious distinction falls to the MAJI committee also known as MAJESTY—a combined council of the heads of the intelligence agencies, along with the president. MJ-12 is a group of consultants to MAJESTY and has never known the whole truth. Information on MJ-12 has been released in order to muddy the waters and obscure the truth about MAJESTY and the MAJI committee, the groups that really run Project Grudge.

THE UNUSUAL SUSPECTS

The Elder Race

MJ-12 and the UFO story are only a cleverly constructed decoy to divert attention away from the real source of mankind's advances in science over recent years: technology recovered from the ruins of an advanced Elder Race that was wiped out by a massive global catastrophe. Those behind the conspiracy want to hide the truth—both of humanity's origins and the fact that we may also one day share the fate of the Elder Race.

MOST CONVINCING EVIDENCE

Defense Secretary James Forrestal was allegedly one of the original members of MJ-12. Shortly after Roswell, he appeared to have a mental breakdown, though few conspiriologists believe that he leapt through a window to his death from the sixteenth floor of a hospital, as was officially claimed. Especially as his personal journals—which were seized by the government—are still classified above top secret after fifty years.

MOST MYSTERIOUS FACT

The aliens who allegedly signed a treaty with MJ-12 claim that they have been genetically tinkering with humanity for millennia. They created Jesus Christ and have used a tachyon scanner that can view images from any time in history, to show his crucifixion. This time-movie has been recorded onto video, and the aliens hold its release in reserve, should they want to cause spiritual chaos.

SKEPTICALLY SPEAKING

While occasional documents have been found to back up the information regarding MJ-12 and its various projects, almost all this evidence includes errors. The people who suggest that the documents were deliberately made to look suspicious when first created, in order to minimize damage if they were leaked, are forgetting the fact that when first written, the supposed authors would have had no reason to know that such an elaborate conspiracy would ever be necessary.

7 THE ODESSA

The popular belief, reinforced by countless war movies and other forms of corporate-controlled media, is that the Allied forces at the end World War II soundly defeated the Nazi Party. The evil had been vanquished, never to rise again. Or did many Nazis not only escape the grasp of the Allies, but also actually receive help from them? Could the Third Reich still be exerting influence over the world? Yes, according to the theories surrounding the Odessa.

Midway through World War II, sensing the way the wind was blowing, many Nazis (among them Otto Skorzeny, Reinhard Gehlen, and Martin Bormann) began to take steps to ensure their own survival. This metaphorical lifeboat was called the Odessa.

The Odessa split into three divisions. The first division, headed by Skorzeny, developed a system for smuggling important members of the Nazi Party to safe havens across

John F. Kennedy is pictured with Allen Dulles, the head of the CIA who allegedly used American tax dollars to employ former Nazis as spies.

the world, including places like Indonesia and South America. The second division, the brainchild of Gehlen (who had been head of Nazi intelligence during World War II) was an organization of Nazi spies that would set up shop in Munich and in time call itself "the Org." The third division handled perhaps the most crucial element in Nazi survival: the transport of money and gold, stolen from Nazi victims, out of a fallen Germany. This was also the work of Skorzeny.

Former Nazi Otto Skorzen was released by the United States in 1947 without facing war crime charges.

But such grandiose plans, no matter how clever and ruthless the perpetrators, would not have succeeded without help. And here the tale of the Odessa takes a much darker turn. It appears that this help came from the United States. In fact, it can be argued that without Nazi intervention, the CIA would never have existed and NASA would never have made it to the moon. Perhaps the Nazi dream did not die—it may have simply changed address.

THE STRANGE PART

Captured by Allied forces, Otto Skorzeny did not face a war crimes tribunal, as would have befitted a Nazi war criminal. Instead, the Americans released him in 1947.

THE USUAL SUSPECTS

The OSS/CIA

Following the war, Allen Dulles of the OSS (Office of Strategic Services) in the United States contracted the spy services of Gehlen, blatantly ignoring the U.S. law that made the employment of Nazis illegal. Using American tax dollars (rumored to be around $200 million), Gehlen polished his ring of Nazi spies into the Org. Then, working alongside Dulles, who later became head of the newly formed CIA in 1947, Gehlen was in a position to manipulate American domestic and foreign policy.

The U.S. Government

Under the notorious Project Paperclip, in which the U.S. government tried to snag German scientists of the Reich for its own programs, several acts of subterfuge and moral laxity were committed. One of the chief beneficiaries of this breaking of American law was NASA, which acquired the services of Wehrner von Braun, a force behind the dreaded V-2 rocket, to work on its space program.

THE UNUSUAL SUSPECTS

The New World Order

The Nazi regime may have been the forerunner of the New World Order, with Adolf Hitler set to conquer the world with the aid of several corporations. But as Hitler proved too unstable, he was removed from his position of power through an inglorious suicide, and the Reich was dramatically dismantled. As the dark forces behind the NWO settled down to wait for another opportunity to realize their dream, they took steps to ensure that their more loyal servants would still be available to continue the work.

MOST CONVINCING EVIDENCE

After being caught by American forces, Gehlen bargained for his freedom by offering microfilm copies of everything that his Nazi intelligence service had gleaned about Russia. The United States made a deal with Gehlen for the microfilm and removed his name from the lists of Nazi POWs in American hands.

MOST MYSTERIOUS FACT

Allen Dulles's older brother, John Foster Dulles, besides being secretary of state in the Eisenhower administration, also acted as American liaison to IG Farben, a chemical company that not only supported the Nazi Party, but even had a plant in Auschwitz itself. Farben made the Zyklon-B crystals that were used in Auschwitz's gas chambers.

SKEPTICALLY SPEAKING

War is a lot like organized sports today—if your team is losing far too often, you just get out of your contract and become free agents. New boss . . . same as the old boss. Given how much is known about what became of certain Nazis it seems unlikely that any organized conspiracy was in operation. The power of the Odessa has been exaggerated.

8 THE TEMPLARS

The First Crusade of the forces of Western Christendom to reclaim the holy sites of Palestine from Muslim forces took place between 1095 and 1099 CE. By the end of the war, the holy city of Jerusalem had been captured and the Kingdom of Jerusalem had been created. The Knights Templar were a monastic order that came into being some time around 1120 in Jerusalem in order to provide protection to the pilgrims from Europe visiting the Holy Land. Founded by a group of nine French knights, the order's full title was the Poor Knights of Christ and of the Temple of Solomon. Within a few decades, the group grew substantially and became an officially sanctioned Christian order backed by the pope and by the combined monarchs of Europe.

The order's sponsor, and the man who drew up the codes of conduct and oaths of poverty that the members followed, was Cistercian abbot Saint Bernard of Clairvaux. He was the chief spokesman of united Christendom and often called "the Second Pope." Because of members' vows of poverty and the donations they took from the wealthy pilgrims they escorted, the

Templars quickly became rich. With wealth came power, and back in Europe after the Crusades, the influence of the Knights Templar grew. Pope Innocent II had exempted the Templars from all authority other than that of the papacy, so they were exempt from law. This same immunity allowed them to practice usury—lending of money for interest—and they became major financiers to European kings. In the process, they created a structure that would later become the banking and finance industry.

Perhaps making use of their legal immunities, the Templars held secret meetings and rituals at which the business of the order was conducted. The truth of what went on at these meetings has long been debated, but whether it was Satanic worship or financial strategic discussions, the end was the same. By the start of the fourteenth century, King Philip "the Fair" of France was deeply in debt to the Templars. Rather than repay them, he chose to conspire with the pope, Clement V, who resented Templar influence. On October 13, 1307, Philip had the Templars arrested for heresy, which allowed him to seize all their funds and torture the knights into confessing to a variety of bad deeds, including demon worship, possession of occult powers, trampling the cross, and sodomy. On March 22, 1312, the order was formally dissolved by Clement V's papal bull entitled "Vox in Excelso."

THE STRANGE PART

It has long been held that Freemasonry was formed from the dying embers of the Knights Templar. Many Templars fled from Europe to Scotland, where the order was not suppressed. It is suspected that the order survives to the present day, both within Freemasonry and separate to it as an individual organization. Long used to manipulating governments and finance, the Templars have kept light hold on the reins of power and still sit in the background of Western society, waiting for the right moment to reveal themselves again.

THE USUAL SUSPECTS

The Freemasons

There is a fair amount of evidence to link the Templars to the Freemasons. Several Masonic degrees and rites draw explicitly on Templar imagery and even use Templar titles. Given that the order fled to Scotland and that there is a Scottish Rite (or branch; the three Rites are theoretically separate organizations) of Freemasonry, the Templars could well have become the Freemasons, which would leave them still in power at the beginning of the twenty-first century.

THE UNUSUAL SUSPECTS

The Assassins

The famed Assassins of the Middle East were the fighting force of the Ismaeli Sect of Islam, ruled today by the Aga Khan. Known to work via infiltration, the Assassins may have compromised the Knights Templar during the Crusades as a way of gaining a foothold in the Western world—a foothold on which they have been building ever since.

MOST CONVINCING EVIDENCE

One of the most compelling pieces of evidence for the continued existence of the Templars is the Templar Research Institute, part of a mysterious group known as CIRCES International Inc., a non-profit fraternal charity. According to its charter, the Templar Research Institute is dedicated to chivalry, but conspiracy theorists—as usual—have their doubts.

MOST MYSTERIOUS FACT

On March 19, 1314, the last grand master of the Knights Templar, Jacques de Molay, was burned at the stake. As he died, he cursed King Philip and Pope Clement, telling them that they would join him within the year. The pope died within five weeks of the prediction, and Philip died within eight months.

SKEPTICALLY SPEAKING

There is no need to look any deeper into the mystery of the Templars than the obvious facts. A greedy king and an unscrupulous pope wanted to get rid of their enemies, so they trumped up a load of charges and tortured the Templars for confessions, then shut the order down.

9 THE TRIADS

Trading on the images of blood oaths, mysterious rituals, and the Death of a Thousand Knives, the Triads— Chinese criminal organizations—have a rather exotic reputation. Like several other criminal organizations, they arose as rebellious conspiracies to overthrow unpopular, restrictive, or invading governments. Triads have one of the longest pedigrees of all the crime organizations. Triads have their roots in a precursor, imaginatively named "the Red Eyebrows," that was founded during the first century BCE to overthrow the Han dynasty.

The first proper Triad organization—that is, the first one that can be traced directly through to the current day—was the Hung League, which arose during the seventeenth century. Also called the Heaven and Earth Society, it was supposedly founded by five monks for the purpose of rebelling against the Chi'ing dynasty and returning power to the Ming dynasty. Many other rebellious criminal secret societies arose during the eighteenth and nineteenth centuries, but most of their energies went towards organizing criminal activities against the common citizens, rather than encouraging antigovernmental terrorism.

In modern China and Hong Kong, the Triads are extremely active but are more often visible as small-scale gangs rather than large entities run by criminal masterminds. They provide muscle and expertise at street level, running small extortion, prostitution, and forgery rings; fencing stolen goods; and distributing drugs on a day-to-day basis. Before a major government clampdown in 1956, the Triads had been much more organized, with a comparatively rigid control structure, treaties, and some degree of cooperation.

Emigration from Hong Kong and Taiwan allowed the Triads to set up in the United Kingdom and in America. Government reports have assessed that, although much of the crime in the Asian communities in both countries is linked to the Triads, they are not controlled from Hong Kong or China. However, such findings might well be prompted by vested interests; neither the British nor the American governments want to admit to yet another powerful, organized crime body operating on their territory, and it is also in the interests of the Triads that they should be severely underestimated.

THE STRANGE PART

Despite protestations that there is little central organization, there is a serious Triad-related problem across the United

The influence of the Triads has followed emigrating Chinese communities across the world.

Kingdom and the United States with forged credit cards. It appears that Triad members terrorize vulnerable waiters in Chinese restaurants into copying credit card details from customers paying for a meal. These card details are then shipped to a central source and passed back to the Far East, where forged credit cards are manufactured in bulk using the stolen details and then passed for worldwide distribution. This sort of coordination would be tricky to achieve if the Triads were as fragmented and as preoccupied with infighting as government reports suggest they are.

THE USUAL SUSPECTS

The Network

It is feared that following the handover of Hong Kong to China, the Triads have moved out into the world at large. It is thought that from their new operational headquarters in Australia, the Triads have joined with the Yakuza, the Tongs, the Mafia, and the IRA to extort money on a grand scale from governments and major corporations, partly through electronic terrorism such as viruses and hacker scares.

THE UNUSUAL SUSPECTS

Japan

When the Japanese invaded China in the 1930s, they paid the Triads to work for them. Even though the Communists under Mao Tse Tung eventually won, the Japanese government paid the Triads in Hong Kong (through an organization called the Lee Yuen Company) to police the residents and suppress any anti-Japanese activity. The Japanese government may still be the force behind Triad activity today.

MOST CONVINCING EVIDENCE

Although the theft and redistribution of fake credit cards is well documented in England, the extent can be quite shocking. One restaurant in Birmingham was found to be the source of nineteen incidents of credit card duplication (with subsequent fraudulent transactions) in the Far East in just fourteen days, which suggests a very well-polished organizational structure.

MOST MYSTERIOUS FACT

In one well-publicized interview of a notorious Triad enforcer, known as BC, by the journalist Terry Gould, several allegations were made about the scope of gang activities. BC revealed that there is a large Triad organization called the Big Circle and said that it consisted of several sections. There were so many members of the Big Circle, in fact, that many of them did not know that they were part of the same organization. There is a degree of debate as to whether the Big Circle was just a large Triad, like the 14K, which is known to have several subsidiary groups, or whether it was an overarching unifying power, dictating policy and action.

SKEPTICALLY SPEAKING

Although the case for central organization is quite persuasive, given the endemic violence between rival Triad groups, it seems more likely that the apparent cooperation is merely one small skein of mutual interest. In most matters, on a day-to-day basis, the Triads remain a collection of petty gangs, operating under a common name purely because of the fear the Triad name can cause.

10 THE KGB

For many observers, the true death knell of the Soviet Union was heard in 1991 when an enthusiastic crowd toppled the statue of Felix Dzerzhinsky and the air resounded with the sound of it shattering into hundreds of pieces. For years his figure had looked across the square that bore his name towards the infamous headquarters of the KGB—the Lubyanka.

Dzerzhinsky was the mastermind behind the Red Terror that allowed the Communists to seize and hold on to power after the overthrow of the czar in the 1917 October Revolution. He created the Cheka secret police that over the years mutated into the Committee of State Security—more commonly known by the initials KGB—the most dreaded and pervasive intelligence-gathering network the world has ever seen.

The KGB (Komitet Gosudarstvennoy Bezopasnosti) was responsible for defending the Soviet Communist regime against internal and external enemies. When the statue of its founder was destroyed, it was symbolic of the breaking of the hold the KGB had on every Soviet citizen, a hold that was maintained from cradle to grave. During the Cold War, wherever there was a hint of conspiracy, there was also a rumor of KGB involvement. Some conspiracy buffs believe that the world's largest covert organization did not even owe allegiance to Communism, but existed only to serve its own mysterious ends.

In theory, the KGB was responsible to the Soviet Council of Ministers; in practice it took its orders directly from the USSR's ruling politburo, if it took orders at all. With the collapse of the Soviet Union and the dismantling of the KGB in 1991, commentators were quick to describe the organization as "lost to history." Some conspiriologists are not so certain that the KGB's awesome, globe-spanning power has been brought to an end.

To many it seemed suspicious that the KGB—which had controlled the Soviet population using fear and an extensive network of secret informers—had allowed the USSR to collapse with barely a pretense of opposition, particularly as the KGB had a supervisory influence on the Soviet army. Conspiracy theorists believe that the apparent end of the Soviet Union and the KGB was merely a cover for an insidious KGB plot to consolidate its power and bring about an even stronger Russian empire.

Vladimir Putin, the current Russian president, is just one of many Russian politicians who were former agents of the KGB.

THE STRANGE PART

Since the fall of the Soviet Union, Russia has been sliding into anarchy. One of the main beneficiaries of this has been Vladimir Zhironovsky, leader of the extreme nationalist Liberal Democratic Party. Millions of Russians have agreed with his statement that "What Russia needs now is a dictator, when I come to power I will be that dictator," and voted for him in presidential and parliamentary elections.

With links to ultra-right groups in Germany, to the Russian Mafia, and even to Saddam Hussein, Zhironovsky is a potential

Russian Hitler with a huge arsenal of nuclear weaponry at his disposal—an arsenal he has threatened to use. Perhaps the most worrying fact is that Zhironovsky was a secret KGB agent. Some of his former associates claim he is being prepared for power by the ex-leaders of the allegedly disbanded secret police and espionage agency.

THE USUAL SUSPECTS

Bavarian Illuminati

Even some orthodox historians are beginning to recognize the key role that several secret societies and occult orders had on the creation of Nazi Germany and Hitler. Behind many of these groups is the specter of the Bavarian Illuminati, whose modus operandi is to stay in the shadows, take control of other clandestine organizations, and then work through them. Could the Illuminati have followed an age-old pattern and subverted the KGB? Given that Zhironovsky has close links to German right-wing groups with fascist origins it could be that the hand of the Illuminati is controlling the KGB and the Russian Hitler-in-waiting.

Freemasons

It is well established that the KGB infiltrated Masonic organizations as part of its attempt to place its agents in the British government and security services. However, it is suspected that the traffic was two-way and that the Freemasons penetrated deep within the leadership of the Committee of State Security and managed to take control of it. Some conspiracy theorists now feel the KGB and its plans to recreate a Russian Empire are merely part of a larger Masonic plot to achieve world domination.

THE UNUSUAL SUSPECTS

Teutonic Knights

The Germanic protégés of the Knights Templar, the Teutonic Knights, once controlled the independent principality Ordensland, which covered Finland, Prussia, and large tracts of Russia. Once they lost their powerbase in the fourteenth century, the Teutonic Knights became a secret society determined to regain the lost lands. Some conspiriologists believe that the Teutonic Knights were the hidden power behind the czars and, that when the Russian royal family became hard to control, masterminded the revolution and infiltrated the new secret police. In this conspiracy scenario, the Teutonic Knights staged the disintegration of the USSR and the KGB in order to form a fascist state that would have more popular support and therefore be easier to control.

MOST CONVINCING EVIDENCE

Former president of the Soviet Union Mikhail Gorbachev denies the accusation made by some conspiracy theorists that he instructed the KGB to create Zhironovsky's Liberal

Democratic Party. However, he does admit the possibility that the former secret police are controlling Zhironovsky. Gorbachev has stated, "Can the KGB create a whole party? Zhironovsky is a remarkable actor; it is very important to find out who is directing him, who is behind him."

MOST MYSTERIOUS FACT

When Russian voters backed Vladimir Putin as president, they were voting for another KGB creation. While not so extreme as Zhironovsky, he is a former spy who also headed the Federal Security Service, the official successor of the KGB. Often seen on TV practicing the martial art prowess that comes from KGB training, no one has discovered his exact role within the KGB between 1975 and 1989. However, Putin has spoken more than once of the need for a "dictatorship of the law," and some see his rule as being merely a KGB dry run before Zhironovsky is installed.

SKEPTICALLY SPEAKING

There is very little solid evidence of the KGB surviving the disbanding process. History shows that anti-Semitism and severe economic woe are sometimes all the reasons that are needed to explain the rise of a megalomaniac, would-be world dictator.

11 M16

MI6 is known across the globe as the British security service responsible for defending the realm from external enemies, thanks to its portrayal as the employer of Special Agent 007 in the decade-spanning series of hit James Bond movies. However, in the shadows where conspiracy theories thrive, there are many who see MI6's portrayal in the films as a force for good as no more than blatant propaganda. MI6, they feel, is an organization that is secretly dedicated to achieving world domination.

In theory, MI6 is neutral and does not align itself to any particular political party or ideology. Even the most hardened skeptic viewing modern history would have to admit that one thing MI6 could not be accused of is being neutral. There are many established examples of MI6 campaigning against a politician or organization that it feels is too left wing or that does not support the "special relationship" between Britain

Elements of MI6 worked to force Prime Minister Harold Wilson out of office. They succeeded in 1976.

and America. The most famous case is the removal of Prime Minister Harold Wilson from power.

It had long been rumored that MI6, in conjunction with its sister service MI5, had been behind the sudden resignation of Wilson in 1976. When the government was unable to prevent the publication of ex-MI5 agent Peter Wright's memoirs, the full details of the conspiracy to remove Wilson in a bloodless coup eventually became public knowledge. The devastating allegations point to a treasonable conspiracy undertaken by a cabal of intelligence officers to undermine and bring down the constitutionally elected government of the United Kingdom.

There are also many other cases of MI6 blackmailing, smearing, and recruiting members of Parliament—not an activity the movies have ever portrayed James Bond undertaking as part of his remit to "defend the realm." One of the key figures seen to be involved with MI6's ongoing attempt to subvert its own nation's democracy was director of CIA counter-intelligence James Jesus Angleton—mastermind of the Italian P2 conspiracy, possible mastermind of the Kennedy assassination, and a member of the mysterious Knights of Malta.

Confirmed conspiratorial actions against the British government, undertaken with allies from the American intelligence community, have made many conspiracy theorists wonder just who MI6 actually works for. If MI6 is not loyal to democratically elected British leaders, they feel it may be engaged as a key player in a conspiracy to achieve global domination for a secret Anglo-American cabal.

THE STRANGE PART

There is no doubting that a network of "Atlanticist" groups exist and work behind the scenes of international politics. These round-table groups often share a common membership, which suggests that the American Council on Foreign Relations works closely with British groups such as the Royal Institute of International Affairs. Given that the leadership of MI6 and the CIA play a prominent role in all of these groups,

James Bond—the acceptable face of MI6—was invented by former British spy Ian Fleming to create a better image for the secret service.

conspiriologists feel that it is not unfair to suspect the security services are working to a secret agenda on behalf of these organizations.

THE USUAL SUSPECTS

The Royal Family

More than one conspiracy buff has pointed the finger at the royal family as the cement that bonds the alleged

Anglo-American cabal. They believe that the royal family has been working since the nineteenth century to promote the doctrine of "mystical imperialism" and world domination by the two largest English-speaking nations. Early steps in this process included inspiring Cecil Rhodes to set up round-table groups and the Rhodes scholarships at Oxford, which would mean the brightest Americans—including President Bill Clinton—received their "education" in England. MI6 swears loyalty to the Crown, so its part in the conspiracy comes from following the direct orders of the queen.

Rockefeller Family

The Rockefellers are one of the most fabulously wealthy families in the world and seem to be major players in the conspiracies behind international politics. With possible controlling interests in several banks and major corporations, including the Federal Reserve Bank, which controls all money in the United States, David Rockefeller is also chairman of both the Trilateral Commission and the Council on Foreign Relations. Some conspiracy theorists believe that the Rockefellers' aim is to create a superpower Anglo-American alliance dedicated to preserving and furthering their financial interests.

THE UNUSUAL SUSPECTS

Rosicrucians

The origins of the Order of the Rose Cross are a matter of heated debate in conspiracy circles. Whether they developed from an ancient Egyptian cult or were the idea of Giordano Bruno—a sixteenth-century philosopher burned for organizing secret societies and teaching that life existed on other planets— there is no doubting the Rosicrucians are major conspiracy players. Given that they infiltrated British Freemasonry centuries ago, it is not impossible that they are the true controllers of the Anglo-American cabal.

Knights of Malta

Operating out of small office in the Vatican, the Knights of Malta have included members as diverse as General Reinhard Gehlen, Hitler's chief of intelligence, who later worked for the CIA; and General Alexander Haig, the force behind Nixon's and Reagan's foreign policies and a friend of the queen's. Some conspiriologists feel the Knights of Malta secretly control the CIA and via that organization, MI6. Just why the Knights of Malta would want to do this is open to question, but it is known that the Knights Templar regard them as their sworn enemies.

MOST CONVINCING EVIDENCE

People looking for evidence of MI6 trying to establish closer ties between Britain and America have turned their attention to the British-American Project. Backed by companies such as American Express, Apple Computers, British Airways, Coca-Cola, Monsanto, and Philip Morris, it is officially a charitable trust that aims to bring together senior representatives from the intelligence services business, government, the media, and the armed forces from the two countries. However, conspiracy theorists feel MI6's alleged links with the project means that it serves a more sinister purpose.

MOST MYSTERIOUS FACT

Recently disclosed British government documents show that there were plans to turn the United Kingdom into the fifty-first state of the United States. Was the real reason MI6 chose to remove Harold Wilson from office because he scrapped these plans?

SKEPTICALLY SPEAKING

It seems unlikely that MI6 is competent enough at covert operations to be capable of masterminding an ultrasecret plot to shape world politics. If the organization can't even prevent itself from being publicly exposed as severely compromised by Soviet intelligence, it is doubtful that MI6 has the ability to successfully run a dozen top-level conspiracy organizations and two major governments.

GLOSSARY

black ops Short for black operations, a term used in politics, the military, intelligence, and business to refer to activities that are secret due to their questionable legal or ethical implications.

cabal A group of people secretly plotting something or united to bring about some form of intrigue.

cartel A combination of independent commercial or industrial enterprises created to limit competition or fix prices.

conspiriologists Conspiracy theorists who have taken an interest in researching the truth behind various dark plots.

edict A proclamation that has the force of law; an order or command.

Elder Race A civilization that was more advanced than our current one, and that predates it.

Illuminati An organization founded in Bavaria in 1776; any underground intellectual movement or secret society. The term is also often used to describe any hidden elite aiming for world domination and possessing enlightenment.

megalomaniac A person with a delusional mental disorder that is marked by feelings of omnipotence and grandeur.

New World Order A new period of history where a dramatic change in political thought and the balance of power occurs worldwide.

papal bull An edict or decree made by the pope, the leader of Roman Catholicism.

P2 Propaganda Due, a Masonic lodge that operated in Italy between 1877 and 1981 and that was implicated in several crimes and mysteries including a bank scandal involving the Vatican.

remit The act of submitting or referring something for consideration, judgment, decision, or action.

subterfuge Deception.

tachyon A hypothetical subatomic particle that always travels faster than the speed of light.

33rd Degree The highest degree of the Scottish rites, conferred by a controlling body of the Freemasons.

Yakuza A loose organization of Japanese criminal organizations and illegal enterprises; the Japanese Mafia.

For More Information

Central Intelligence Agency (CIA)
Office of Public Affairs
Washington, DC 20505
(703) 482-0623
Web site: http://www.cia.gov

Cold War International History Project
Woodrow Wilson Center
One Woodrow Wilson Plaza
1300 Pennsylvania Avenue NW
Washington, DC 20004-3027
(202) 691-4110
Web site: http://www.wilsoncenter.org/index.cfm?topic_id=
    1409&fuseaction=topics.home

Global Policy Forum
777 UN Plaza, Suite 3D
New York, NY 10017
(212) 557-3161
Web site: http://www.globalpolicy.org

The History Channel
Secret Societies episode televised on March 11, 2007
Web site: http://www.history.com

WEB SITES

Due to the changing nature of Internet links, Rosen Publishing has developed an online list of Web sites related to the subject of this book. This site is updated regularly. Please use this link to access the list:

http://www.rosenlinks.com/cm/seso

FOR FURTHER READING

Axelrod, Alan. *The International Encyclopedia of Secret Societies and Fraternal Orders.* New York, NY: Checkmark Books, 1998.

Bondesan, Jan. *The Great Pretenders: The True Stories Behind Famous Historical Mysteries.* New York, NY: W. W. Norton, 2004.

Burnett, Thom, ed. *Conspiracy Encyclopedia: The Encyclopedia of Conspiracy Theories.* New York, NY: Chamberlain Bros., 2005.

Hidell, Al, and Joan D'Arc. *The Complete Conspiracy Reader: From the Deaths of JFK and John Lennon to Government-Sponsored Alien Cover-Ups.* New York, NY: MJF Books, 2003.

Levy, Joel. *The Little Book of Conspiracies: 50 Reasons to Be Paranoid.* New York, NY: Thunder's Mouth Press, 2005.

Reynolds, John Lawrence. *Secret Societies: Inside the World's Most Notorious Organizations.* New York, NY: Arcade, 2006.

Steiger, Brad, and Sherry Steiger. *Conspiracies and Secret Societies: The Complete Dossier.* Detroit, MI: Omnigraphics, 2006.

Tuckett, Kate. *Conspiracy Theories.* New York, NY: Berkley, 2005.

INDEX

PHOTO CREDITS

Cover (*left*), p. 29 Jim Mc Donald/Corbis; cover (*right*), p. 7 Corbis;
p. 12 World Religions Photo Library/Photos12.com; pp. 16, 37, 46, 47
Library of Congress; pp. 19, 57 Stephen Behan/Carlton Books Ltd.;
p. 22 Topham; pp. 34, 69 Collection Cinéman/Photos12.com; p. 41
PressNet/Topham; p. 62 Denis Grishkin/Corbis; p. 67 Bettmann/Corbis.

Designer: Tom Forget